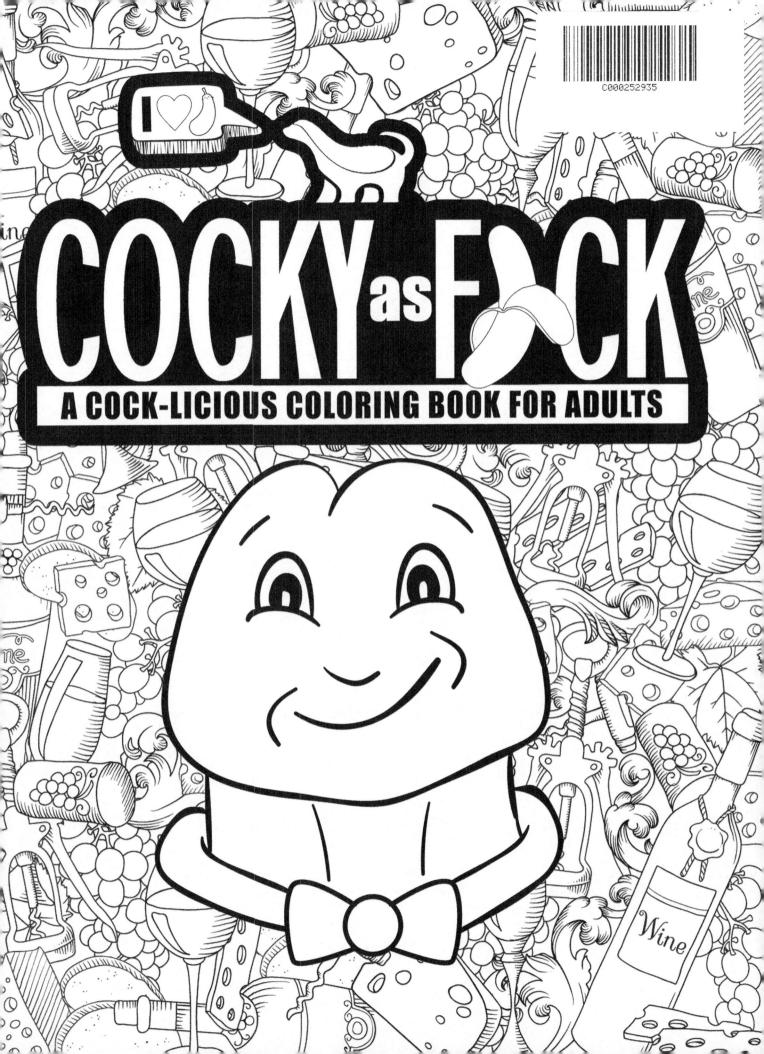

FREE DOWNLOAD!

YOUR CODE: CK3684

www.honeybadgercoloring.com/cocky

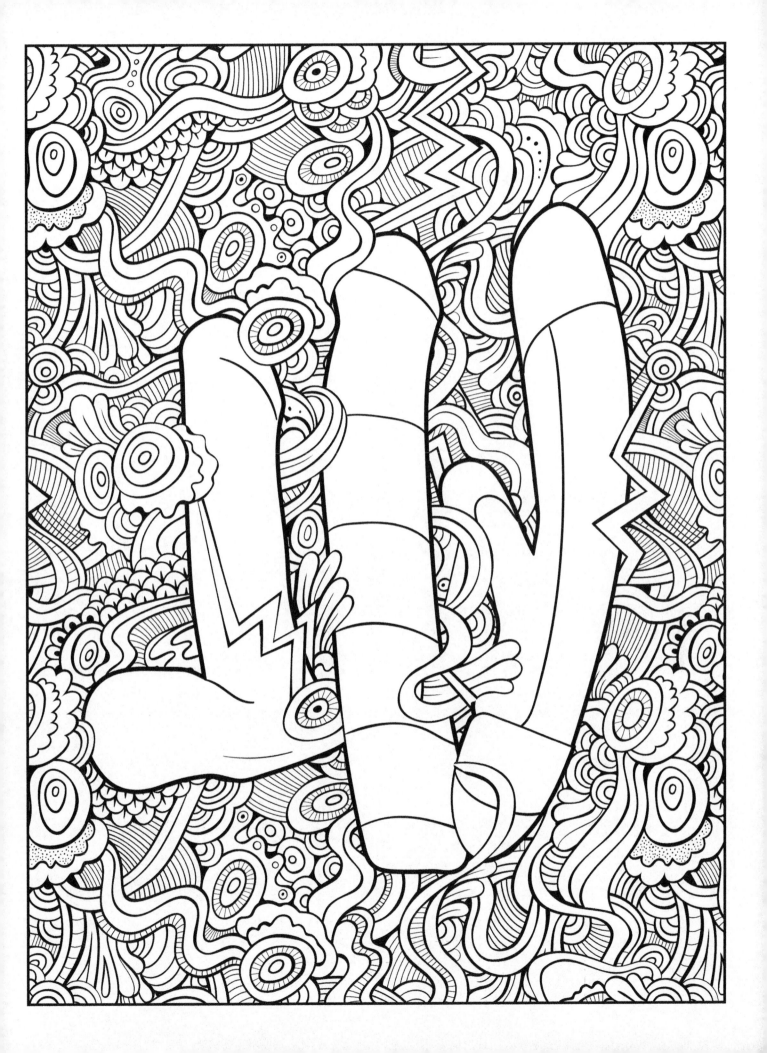

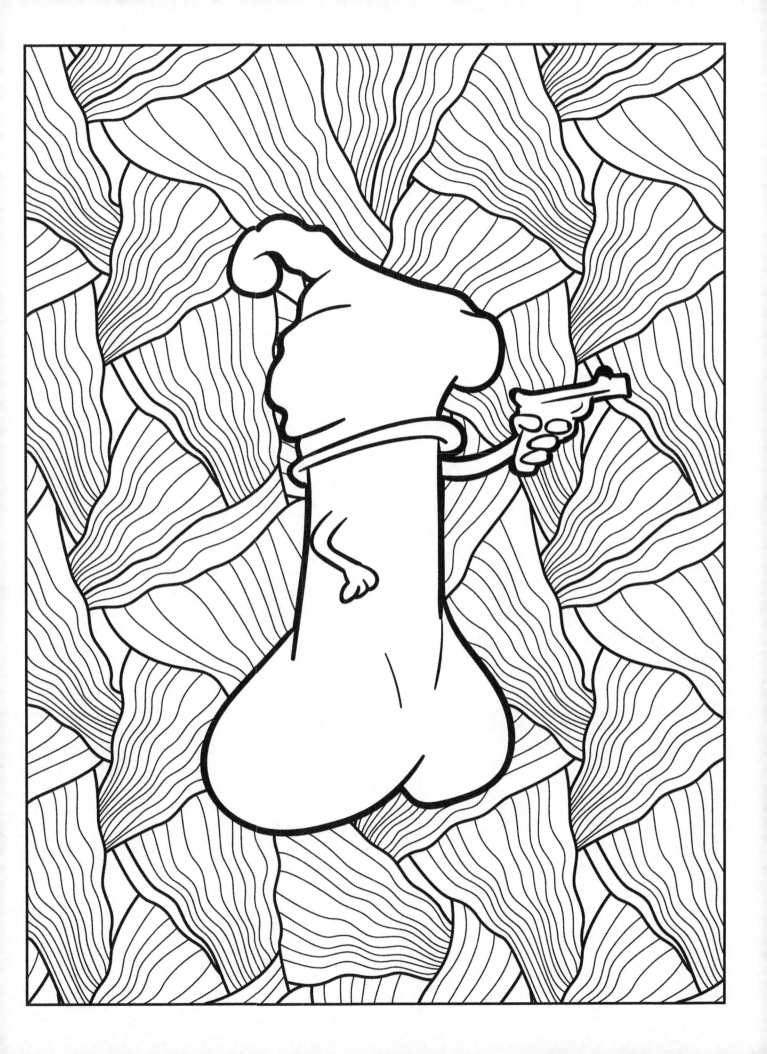

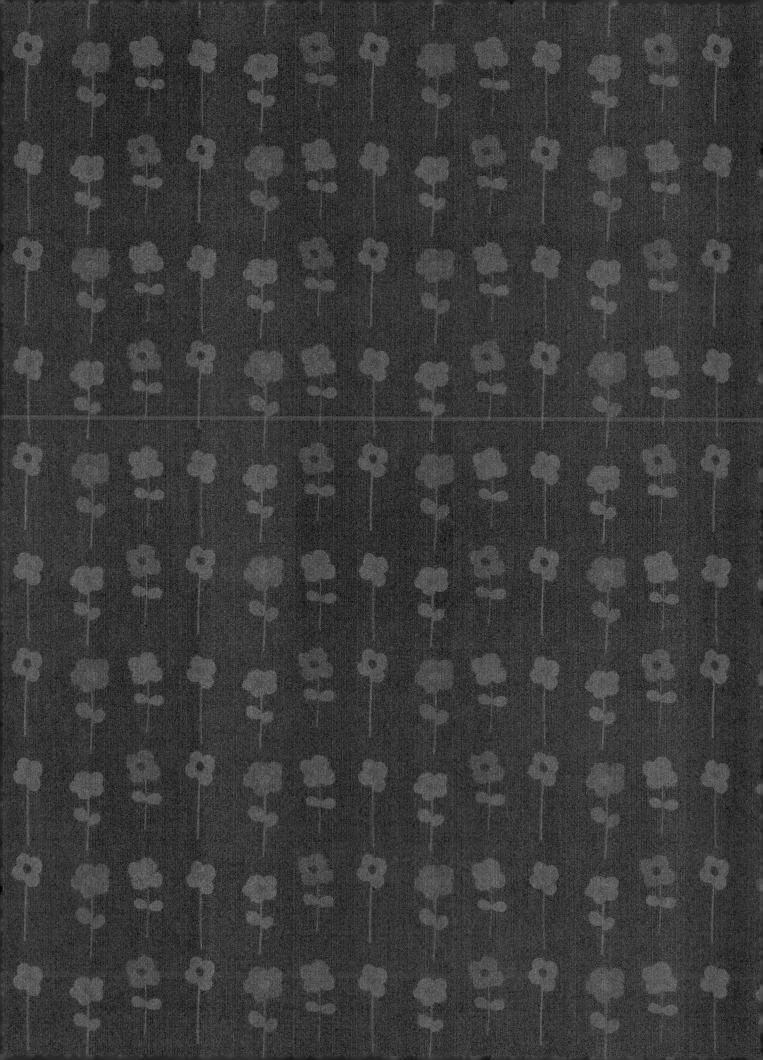

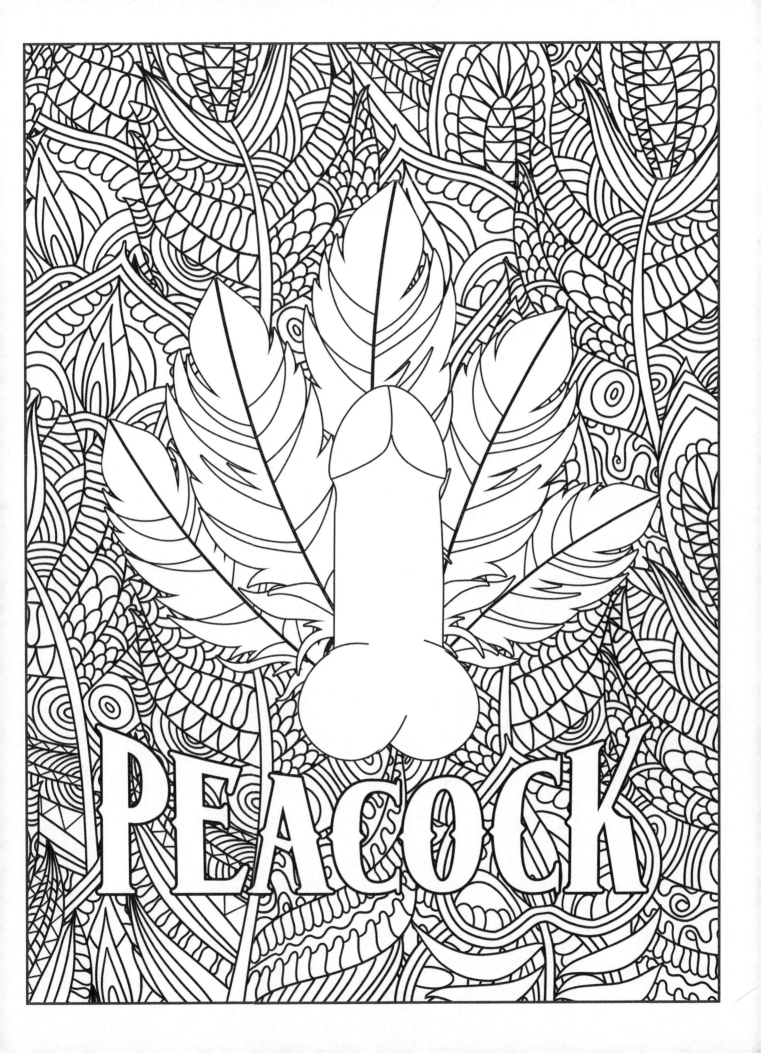

PEACOCK

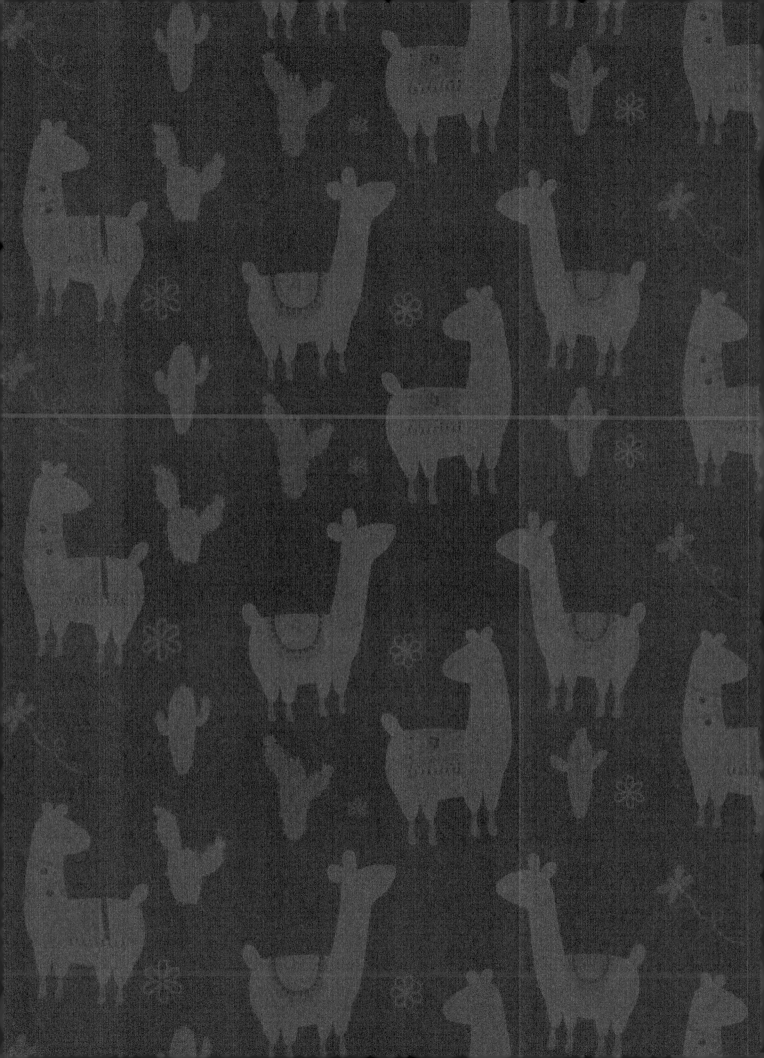

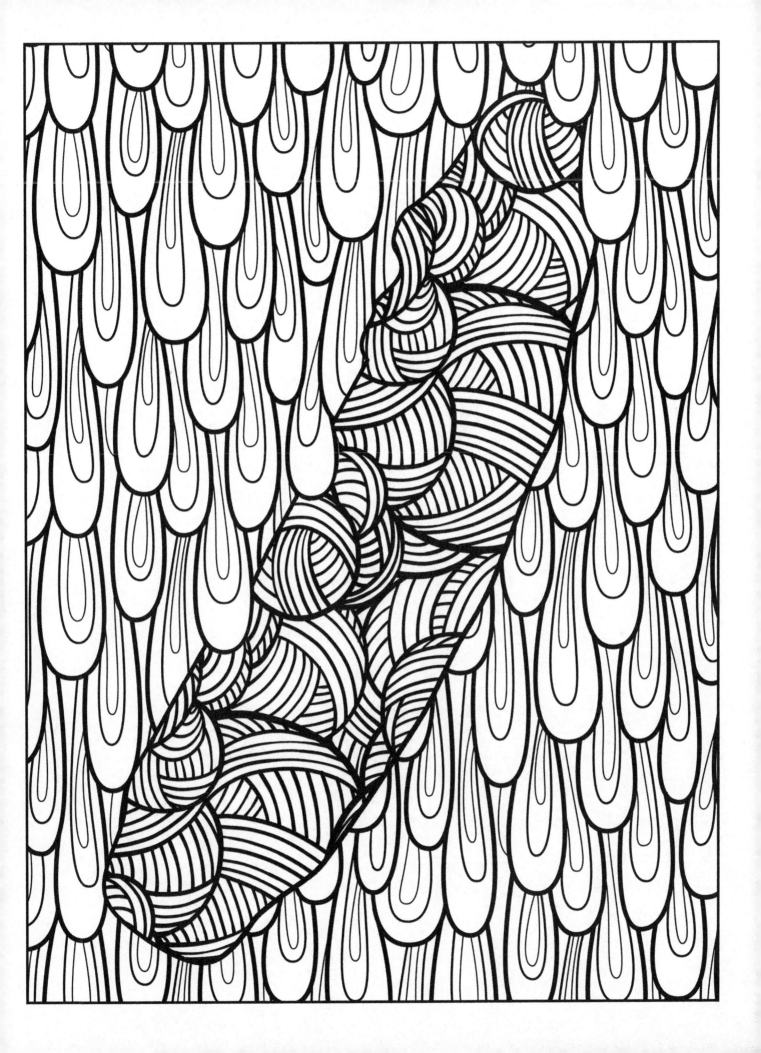

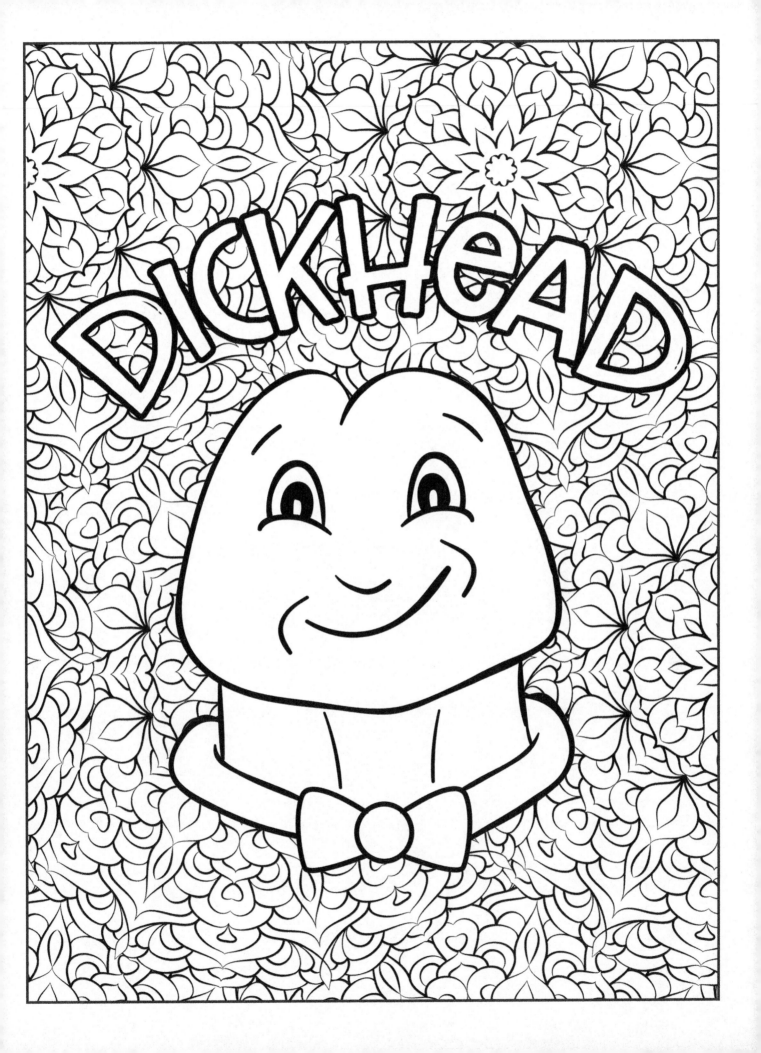

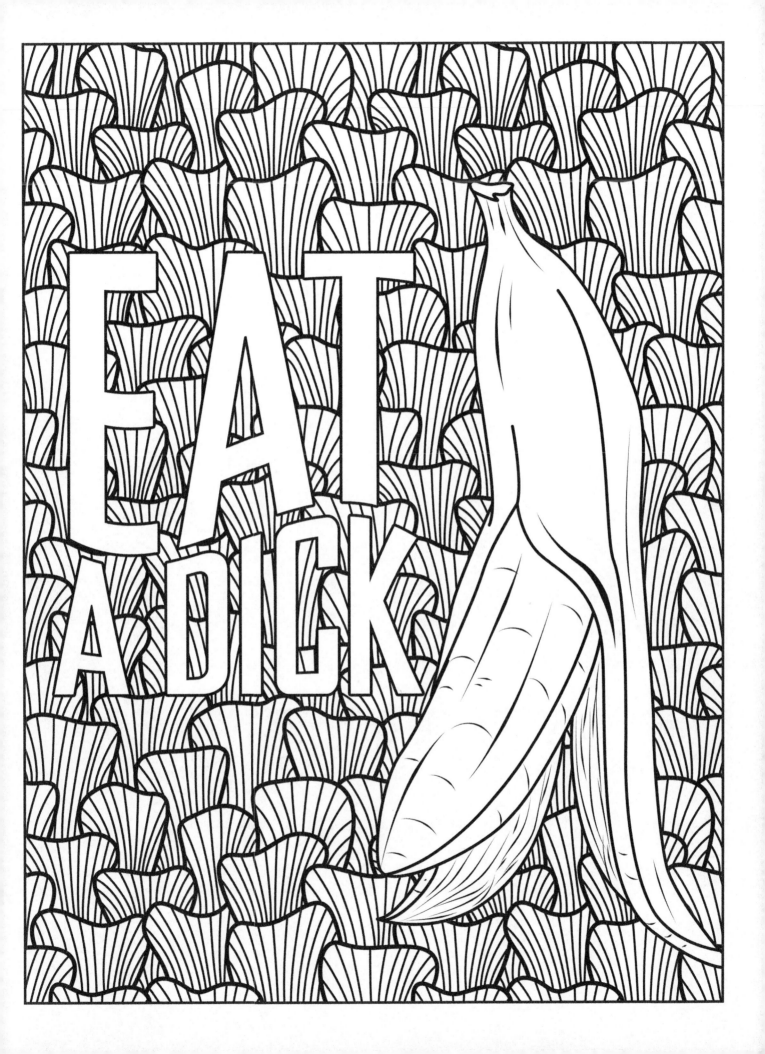

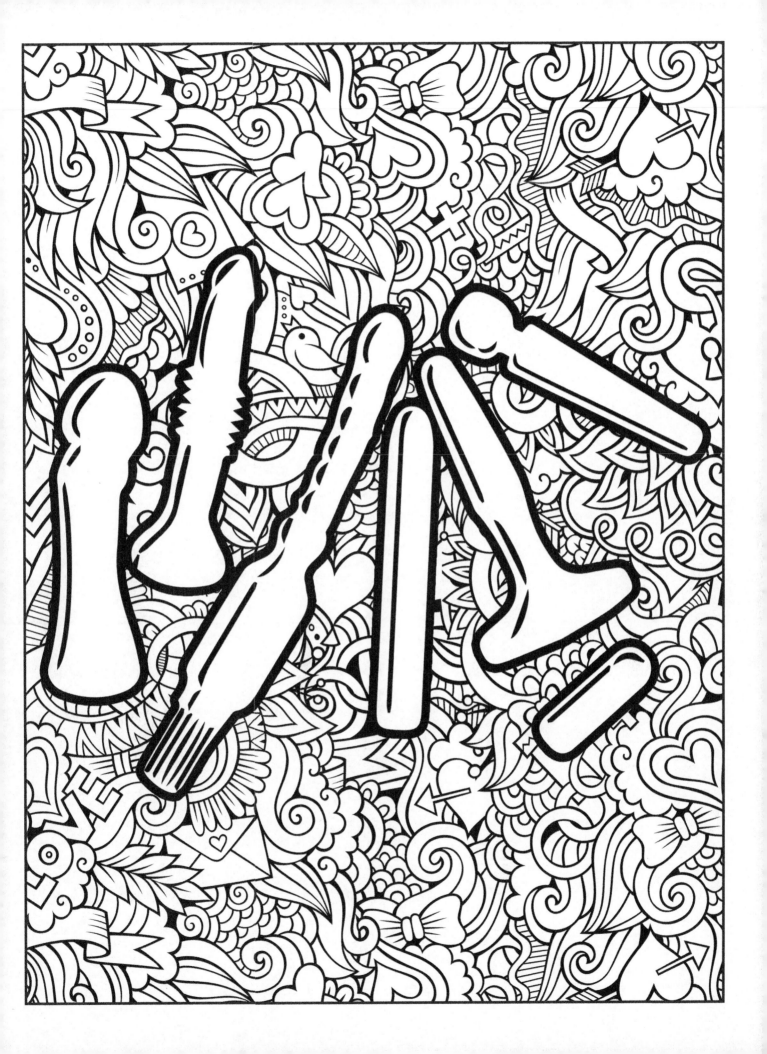

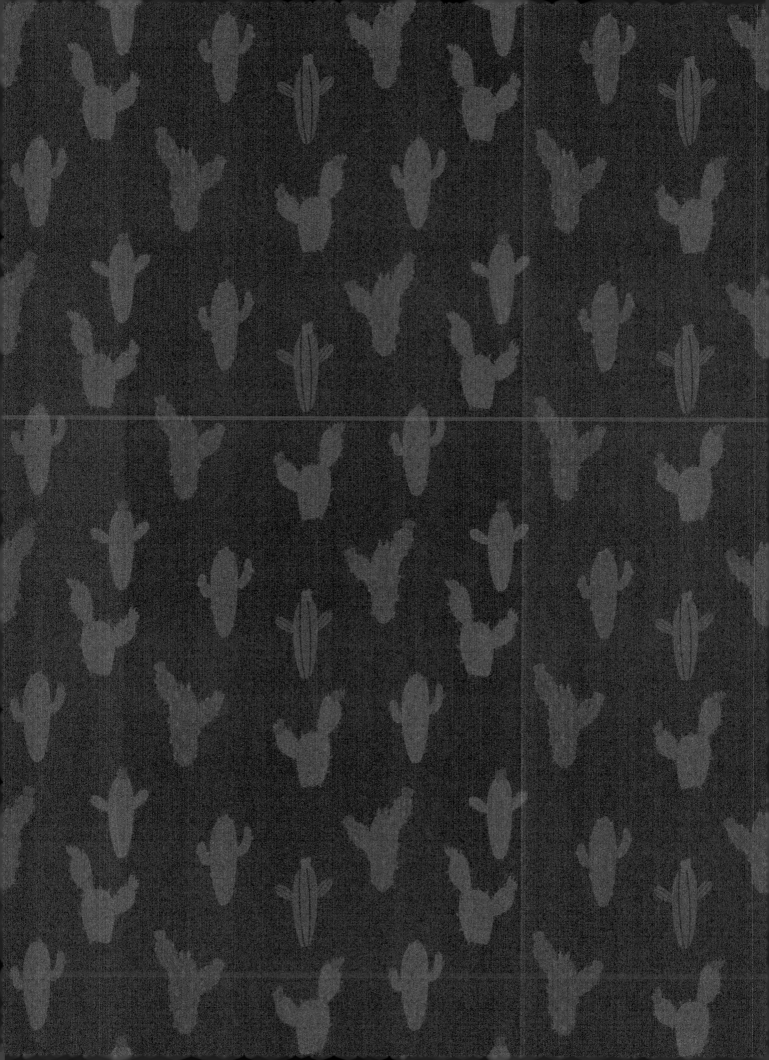

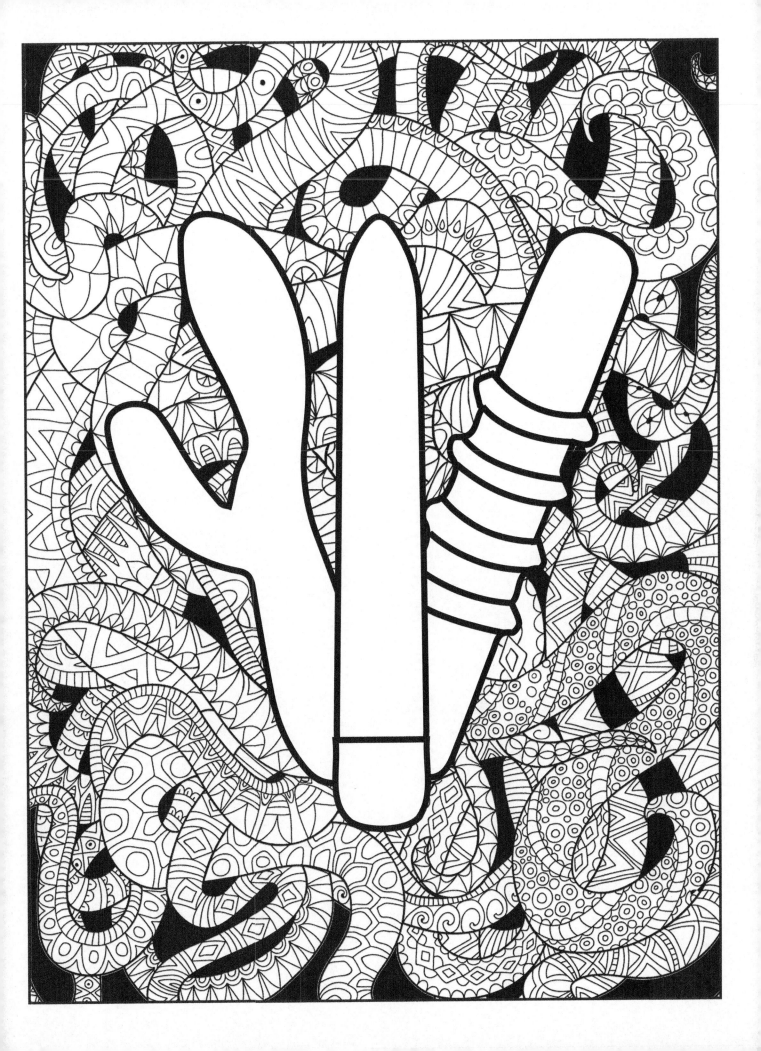

FREE DOWNLOAD!

SON OF A BENCH!

AH, Shirt.

WHAT the FORK?!

YOUR CODE: CK3684

www.honeybadgercoloring.com/cocky

BE SURE TO FOLLOW US
ON SOCIAL MEDIA FOR THE
LATEST GIVEAWAYS & DISCOUNTS

@honeybadgercoloring

Honey Badger Coloring

@badgercoloring

ADD YOURSELF TO OUR MONTHLY
NEWSLETTER FOR FREE DIGITAL
DOWNLOADS AND DISCOUNT CODES

www.honeybadgercoloring.com/newsletter

# CHECK OUT OUR OTHER BOOKS!

www.honeybadgercoloring.com

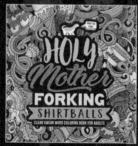
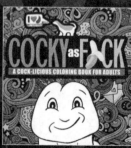

# CHECK OUT OUR OTHER BOOKS!

www.honeybadgercoloring.com

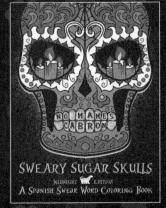
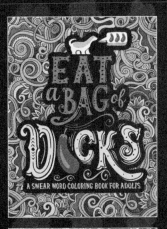

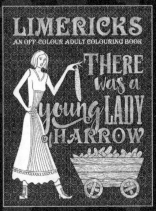

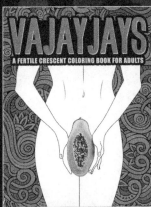

# CHECK OUT OUR OTHER BOOKS!

www.honeybadgercoloring.com

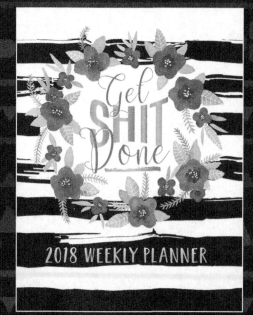